SIDE HUSTLE

MILLIONAIRE

How to Multiply Your Income Tenfold in Five Years

Isabelle Hartley

i

Copyright Copy

All content in this book is protected under copyright laws. Any reproduction, distribution, or unauthorized use of any part of this book without the prior written consent of the copyright owner is strictly prohibited except for personal use.

TABLE OF CONTENT

Introduction

In a world marked by rising living costs and stagnant wages, the pursuit of financial freedom has become a common aspiration. Many individuals, particularly those with limited income from their primary jobs, are seeking innovative ways to secure their financial future. If you find yourself in this situation, you're not alone. The journey from being a low-wage earner to becoming a Side Hustle Millionaire is within your grasp, and this book is your roadmap to achieving that lofty goal.

The Side Hustle Millionaire: How to Multiply Your Income Tenfold in Five Years is not just another self-help book promising overnight success. Instead, it's a practical guide that acknowledges the realities of starting from a modest financial foundation. Whether you're supporting a family, paying off debts, or simply looking for a way to escape the cycle of living paycheck to paycheck, this book is tailored to your needs.

In the following chapters, we'll explore the art and science of launching and scaling profitable side businesses. You'll discover how to leverage your unique skills and interests, identify lucrative opportunities, and set realistic goals. Through careful planning, branding, and marketing, we'll show you how to turn your side hustle into a thriving venture.

Financial management is a crucial aspect of your journey, and we'll delve into budgeting, pricing strategies, and ways to maximize your profits. But it's not just about the money; we'll also address the importance of time management and maintaining a healthy work-life balance.

Throughout this book, you'll find inspiring stories of individuals who started with little more than a dream and transformed their lives through side hustles. These case studies will serve as beacons of hope and motivation, proving that with determination and the right strategies, you can achieve remarkable financial success.

Ultimately, the Side Hustle Millionaire is about more than just making money; it's about gaining the freedom to live life on your terms. So, if you're ready to embark on a transformative journey towards financial independence, turn the page and let's begin the exciting adventure of building your side hustle empire. Your future as a Side Hustle Millionaire starts now.

The Side Hustle Revolution

In the not-so-distant past, the traditional career path was clear-cut: graduate from school, secure a steady job, and climb the corporate ladder. This path was considered the surest way to financial stability and a comfortable life. However, the landscape of employment and income generation has evolved significantly in recent years, giving rise to what can aptly be called the Side Hustle Revolution.

The Side Hustle Revolution represents a fundamental shift in the way people approach work and income. It challenges the conventional wisdom that a single, 9-to-5 job is the only way to secure one's financial future. Instead, it champions the idea that individuals can take control of their earnings by diversifying their income streams through side businesses, freelancing, and entrepreneurial ventures.

But what has sparked this revolution, and why is it gaining momentum at an unprecedented pace? There are several key factors contributing to this seismic shift in the way we think about work and income:

- Economic Uncertainty: The global economy has been characterized by volatility and uncertainty in recent years. Job security is no longer a guarantee, and many individuals have experienced layoffs or downsizing. In response, people are seeking ways to reduce their financial vulnerability by creating alternative sources of income.

- Technological Advancements: The digital age has democratized entrepreneurship. The internet and technology have made it easier than ever to start and market a business, reach a global audience, and automate various aspects of business operations. This accessibility has lowered the barriers to entry for aspiring entrepreneurs.

- Changing Attitudes Towards Work: A growing number of people are reevaluating their relationship with work. They're prioritizing fulfillment, flexibility, and purpose over traditional job security. The desire for work-life balance and the pursuit of passions are driving individuals to explore side hustles that align with their interests.

- Inspiring Success Stories: High-profile success stories of individuals who turned side hustles into multimillion-dollar businesses have captured public attention. These stories serve as inspiration and proof that it's possible to achieve financial independence through entrepreneurial pursuits.

- Millennial Entrepreneurship: The younger generation, particularly millennials, is driving the Side Hustle Revolution. They are more open to risk-taking, value experiences over material possessions, and are tech-savvy, making them well-suited for online businesses and gig economy work.

The Side Hustle Revolution is not just a passing trend; it's a fundamental shift in the way people approach work, income, and financial security. It empowers individuals to take control of their financial destinies, diversify their income sources, and reduce their dependence on traditional employment.

This revolution is inclusive and accessible. It's not limited to a particular age group, education level, or industry. Anyone with a desire to improve their financial situation and a willingness to put in the effort can participate. Whether you're a college student looking to pay off student loans, a parent seeking to provide a better future for your family, or a retiree looking to supplement your pension, the Side Hustle Revolution offers opportunities for everyone.

In the chapters that follow, we'll delve deeper into the strategies and principles that can help you become a part of this revolution. We'll explore how to identify your unique skills and interests, brainstorm profitable side hustle ideas, plan and launch your ventures, and scale them for long-term success. We'll also address the challenges and obstacles you may encounter on your journey and provide real-world examples of individuals who have successfully navigated this new landscape.

The Side Hustle Revolution is not just about making money; it's about reclaiming your financial independence, pursuing your passions, and designing a life that aligns with your values. So, if you're ready to embrace this revolution and embark on a transformative journey toward financial freedom, let's continue on this exciting path of discovery and empowerment. Your future as a Side Hustle Millionaire awaits.

Setting the 10x Income Goal

One of the foundational pillars of achieving success in the Side Hustle Revolution is setting a clear and ambitious income goal. In this chapter, we'll delve into the concept of setting the 10x income goal and why it's a game-changer in the world of side hustles.

Defining the 10x Income Goal

The 10x income goal, as the name suggests, involves aiming to increase your annual income tenfold within a specified timeframe, often five years. While this may initially sound audacious or even impossible, it's a powerful strategy for several reasons.

- Motivation and Ambition: Setting a 10x goal is inherently motivating. It stretches your limits, challenges your beliefs about what's achievable, and ignites a burning desire to take action. When you commit to increasing your income tenfold, you're less likely to settle for small, incremental gains.

- Thinking Bigger: By aiming for a 10x increase, you force yourself to think on a larger scale. It encourages you to explore more ambitious side hustle ideas, invest more time and effort, and seek opportunities with higher earning potential.

- Pushing Boundaries: Achieving a 10x increase often requires stepping out of your comfort zone. You'll need to explore new skills, take calculated risks, and leverage innovative strategies to reach your goal. This can lead to personal and professional growth.

- Buffering for Uncertainty: The business world is unpredictable, and economic conditions can change rapidly. Setting a 10x income goal provides a financial buffer, allowing you to weather unexpected setbacks and economic downturns more effectively.

Crafting Your 10x Income Goal

Crafting a 10x income goal is not about plucking a random number out of thin air; it requires thoughtful consideration and planning. Here's how you can go about it:

- Assess Your Current Situation: Start by evaluating your current income and financial situation. How much do you earn annually from your primary job? What are your monthly expenses? What financial goals do you have for the future, such as buying a home, paying off debt, or saving for retirement?

- Determine Your Timeframe: Decide on a reasonable timeframe for achieving your 10x income goal. Five years is a common benchmark, but you can adjust it based on your circumstances and risk tolerance.

- Factor in Expenses and Taxes: Remember that as your income increases, so do your expenses and potential tax liabilities. Account for these factors when setting your goal to ensure that your increased earnings translate into meaningful financial growth.

- Research Your Market: If your side hustle involves a specific business or industry, research the market to understand its earning potential. Analyze competitors, pricing, and demand to gauge the feasibility of achieving your goal.

- Break It Down: To make the goal more manageable, break it down into smaller milestones. What should your income be at the end of each year to stay on track toward the 10x goal? These interim targets can serve as checkpoints for your progress.

- Adjust and Iterate: Your 10x income goal should be ambitious but also flexible. As you gain experience and insights from your side hustle journey, be willing to adjust and refine your goal to reflect changing circumstances and opportunities.

Overcoming Doubt and Fear

Setting a 10x income goal may trigger doubt and fear. You might question whether it's realistic or worry about failure. It's essential to acknowledge these feelings and understand that they are a natural part of pursuing ambitious goals.

To combat doubt and fear, focus on building your self-confidence, developing a growth mindset, and surrounding yourself with a support system of mentors and peers who believe in your potential. Remember that the Side Hustle Revolution is about taking calculated risks and learning from both successes and setbacks.

In the chapters that follow, we'll explore practical strategies for turning your 10x income goal into a reality. You'll learn how to identify your skills and interests, generate profitable side hustle ideas, and create a plan to achieve your income aspirations. The journey won't be without challenges, but with determination and the right strategies, you can make remarkable progress toward your goal and ultimately join the ranks of Side Hustle Millionaires who have transformed their financial lives.

Chapter 1: Assessing Your Skills and Interests

Before embarking on your journey to become a Side Hustle Millionaire and achieving your 10x income goal, it's crucial to take a deep dive into your own skills and interests. This self-assessment will lay the foundation for a side hustle that not only boosts your income but also aligns with your passions and strengths.

Identifying Your Strengths

In the pursuit of becoming a Side Hustle Millionaire and achieving your 10x income goal, one of the critical steps is identifying your strengths. Your strengths are the unique abilities, skills, and talents that you bring to the table. Recognizing and leveraging these strengths is essential for creating a side hustle that not only generates income but also aligns with your capabilities and passions.

Uncovering Your Core Strengths

Self-Reflection: Begin by taking a moment for introspection. Reflect on your experiences, both personal and professional, and consider the skills that you excel at. What tasks do you find relatively easy to accomplish, and which ones do you enjoy the most?

- Feedback from Others: Sometimes, those around us can provide valuable insights into our strengths. Reach out to friends, family, colleagues, and mentors and ask them what they believe your strengths are. They may highlight skills or talents you hadn't considered.

- Assess Your Achievements: Review your past achievements, whether they're in your job, hobbies, or personal life. What were the skills or qualities that contributed to your success in those situations?

- Personality Assessments: Consider taking personality assessments like the Myers-Briggs Type Indicator (MBTI) or the StrengthsFinder test. These tools can provide insights into your personality traits and strengths.

- Passions and Interests: Think about the activities or subjects that genuinely excite you. Your passions often align with your strengths. For example, if you're passionate about storytelling, your strength might be in creative writing or communication.

Categorizing Your Strengths

Once you've identified your strengths, categorize them to gain a more structured understanding. Common categories include:

- Technical Skills: These are the specific skills you've acquired through education or experience. They could include programming, design, data analysis, or any other specialized knowledge.

- Soft Skills: Soft skills are your interpersonal skills, communication abilities, emotional intelligence, and leadership qualities. These are often just as valuable as technical skills in the world of side hustles.

- Creative Abilities: Creativity encompasses skills like writing, art, music, and innovation. If you find joy and satisfaction in creative pursuits, they can be integral to your side hustle.

- Industry Knowledge: If you have expertise in a particular industry, such as finance, healthcare, or technology, this knowledge can be a significant strength that sets you apart in your side hustle.

- Problem-Solving and Critical Thinking: Your ability to analyze complex problems and devise solutions is a valuable strength, especially if your side hustle involves consulting or problem-solving services.

Leveraging Your Strengths in Your Side Hustle

Once you've identified and categorized your strengths, it's time to leverage them effectively in your side hustle. Here's how:

- Align Your Side Hustle: Choose a side hustle that aligns with your strengths. For example, if you have a knack for graphic design, consider offering freelance design services. If you're a skilled communicator, think about content creation or consulting.

- Skill Enhancement: Invest in further developing your strengths. Take courses, attend workshops, or seek mentorship to continually improve and stay competitive in your chosen field.

- Collaborate: Collaborating with others who complement your strengths can be a powerful strategy. Partnering with someone whose skills complement yours can lead to innovative and successful ventures.

- Marketing Your Strengths: In your marketing materials and when interacting with potential clients or customers, emphasize your strengths. Highlight how your unique abilities can benefit them.

- Continuous Improvement: Regularly assess and reassess your strengths as your side hustle evolves. Adapt to changing market conditions and emerging trends to remain relevant and competitive.

Identifying your strengths is not just about recognizing what you're good at; it's about harnessing those talents to build a side hustle that thrives. Your strengths are your secret weapons on the path to achieving your 10x income goal. In the upcoming chapters, we'll explore how to transform these strengths into profitable side hustle ideas and actionable strategies that can propel you toward financial independence.

Passion vs. Profit: Finding the Right Balance

In the quest to become a Side Hustle Millionaire and achieve your 10x income goal, a critical decision you'll face is whether to prioritize passion or profit in your side hustle. Striking the right balance between these two factors is essential for long-term success and fulfillment.

The Passion-Driven Approach

Passion is a powerful driving force. When you're deeply passionate about your side hustle, work doesn't feel like work; it becomes an enjoyable pursuit. Here's why a passion-driven approach matters:

- Intrinsic Motivation: Pursuing something you're passionate about naturally fuels your intrinsic motivation. You're more likely to dedicate time and effort to your side hustle because you genuinely love what you're doing.

- Resilience: Passion provides the resilience needed to weather challenges and setbacks. When you encounter obstacles, your passion can help you push through and stay committed to your goals.

- Creativity and Innovation: Passion often leads to creativity and innovation. You're more likely to come up with unique ideas and solutions when you're deeply engaged in your side hustle.

- Personal Fulfillment: A passion-driven side hustle can provide a profound sense of personal fulfillment. It aligns with your interests and values, contributing to a more satisfying life overall

- However, there are some considerations to keep in mind when pursuing a passion-driven side hustle:

- Profit Potential: While passion is essential, it's crucial to evaluate the profit potential of your chosen path. Some passions may not translate into lucrative income streams, and you may need to find creative ways to monetize them.

- Market Demand: Assess whether there's a demand for the products or services related to your passion. Passion alone may not be enough to sustain a successful business if there's no market interest.

The Profit-Driven Approach

On the other end of the spectrum is the profit-driven approach, where the primary goal is to maximize earnings. Here's why prioritizing profit can be appealing:

- Financial Stability: A profit-driven side hustle can provide a more immediate and stable source of income, which can be especially important if you have financial obligations or goals.

- Scalability: Profit-driven ventures often have a clear path to scalability. You can reinvest earnings to grow the business, potentially leading to substantial long-term wealth.

- Market Opportunities: A profit-driven approach allows you to identify and capitalize on market opportunities, which may not always align with personal passions but can be highly profitable.
- However, there are potential downsides to a profit-driven approach:
- Burnout: Focusing solely on profit can lead to burnout if you're not passionate about what you're doing. The absence of intrinsic motivation may make it challenging to sustain the effort required.
- Lack of Fulfillment: If your side hustle is solely profit-driven and doesn't align with your interests or values, you may eventually find it unfulfilling, leading to dissatisfaction.

Finding the Right Balance

The ideal approach often lies in finding a balance between passion and profit. Here's how to strike that balance effectively:

- Identify Overlapping Areas: Look for areas where your passions intersect with profitable opportunities. These are the sweet spots where you can find fulfillment and financial success.

- Prioritize Market Demand: While pursuing your passion is essential, be mindful of market demand. Validate your side hustle idea to ensure there's a viable customer base.

- Plan for Growth: As your side hustle grows, consider reinvesting profits to expand and diversify your income streams. This can lead to both financial success and personal fulfillment.

- Flexibility: Be open to adjusting your approach as circumstances change. Your priorities may evolve over time, and it's okay to pivot your side hustle accordingly.

Ultimately, whether you lean more toward passion or profit, the key is to be intentional and aligned with your goals. A successful side hustle should not only boost your income but also enrich your life and help you move closer to your 10x income goal. In the chapters ahead, we'll explore practical strategies for transforming your passions and strengths into profitable side hustle ideas that balance both passion and profit effectively.

Chapter 2: The Side Hustle Idea Generator

Now that you've assessed your skills, identified your strengths, and considered the balance between passion and profit, it's time to dive into the heart of the Side Hustle Millionaire journey: generating innovative side hustle ideas. This phase is where creativity and practicality come together to lay the foundation for your financial future.

Brainstorming Profitable Ideas

Generating profitable side hustle ideas is a creative process that can open doors to financial independence. Whether you're looking to boost your income, escape the paycheck-to-paycheck cycle, or achieve your 10x income goal, brainstorming is the first step in this transformative journey. Here's how to kickstart your idea generation process:

Problem-Solving

One of the most effective ways to come up with side hustle ideas is by addressing real-world problems or challenges. Think about the issues people face in their daily lives, both big and small. These pain points can serve as the foundation for your side hustle. Here's how to get started:

- Identify Pain Points: Pay attention to your own experiences and those of people around you. What frustrations or challenges do you observe? Common pain points include time constraints, lack of convenience, or unmet needs in specific industries.

- Solutions-Oriented Thinking: Once you've identified a problem, focus on finding solutions. Your side hustle could involve

31

creating a product, service, or platform that addresses and resolves these issues.

- Research and Validation: Research the market to ensure that the problem you've identified has a genuine demand. Use online tools, surveys, and forums to gather insights and validate your idea's potential.

Passion Projects

Turning your passions and hobbies into income-generating opportunities is not only fulfilling but can also be highly profitable. Your interests can provide a natural source of motivation and enthusiasm for your side hustle. Here's how to explore this avenue:

- List Your Passions: Make a list of activities and subjects you're genuinely passionate about. It could be anything from photography and fitness to travel and cooking.
- Identify Monetization Opportunities: For each passion, brainstorm ways to monetize

it. Could you offer coaching, sell products related to your passion, or create content that generates ad revenue?

- Evaluate Market Demand: While pursuing your passions is exciting, you should also assess whether there's a market demand for products or services related to your interests. Ensure there's an audience willing to pay for what you offer.

Market Research

Market research is a cornerstone of idea generation. It involves investigating industry trends, consumer behavior, and identifying gaps or opportunities in the market. Here are steps to help you conduct effective market research:

- Online Tools: Utilize online resources like Google Trends, keyword research tools, and industry-specific forums to uncover popular trends and topics.
- Competitor Analysis: Study your potential competitors. What are they doing well, and

where are they falling short? Identifying gaps in their offerings can lead to innovative side hustle ideas.

- Customer Feedback: Engage with your target audience or potential customers. Conduct surveys, interviews, or focus groups to gather insights and understand their pain points and preferences.

- Emerging Markets: Keep an eye on emerging markets and industries. New technologies, lifestyle changes, and societal shifts often create opportunities for innovative side hustles.

Skill Synergy

Your unique skill set can be a goldmine for side hustle ideas. Consider how your skills, whether technical, creative, or analytical, can be leveraged to create value for others. Here's how to explore this approach:

- Inventory Your Skills: Make a comprehensive list of your skills, both hard and soft. Include everything from coding and graphic design to leadership and communication.

- Skill Combinations: Explore how your skills can complement each other. Sometimes, combining two seemingly unrelated skills can lead to groundbreaking ideas. For example, if you're skilled in programming and have a passion for health and fitness, you might develop a fitness app.
- Market Application: Assess the market to determine if there's demand for services or products that align with your skills. Validate your idea's potential by researching competitors and target audiences.

Feedback Loop

Don't underestimate the power of feedback from others. Sharing your side hustle ideas with friends, family, mentors, or potential customers can provide valuable insights and help you refine your concepts. Here's how to utilize this feedback loop:

- Pitch Your Ideas: Present your side hustle ideas to your trusted network. Encourage open and honest feedback. They may offer suggestions, identify potential issues, or confirm the viability of your concepts.

- Online Communities: Join online communities, forums, or social media groups related to your niche or industry. Engage in discussions, share your ideas, and solicit feedback from a broader audience.

- Prototype and Test: If possible, create prototypes or minimum viable products (MVPs) to demonstrate your concept. Testing your idea with real users can provide invaluable insights.

Remember that brainstorming is an iterative process. Don't be discouraged if your first ideas don't immediately lead to a breakthrough. Keep refining, exploring, and experimenting until you find a side hustle idea that resonates with your goals and passions.

In the following chapters, we'll delve deeper into how to develop, plan, and launch your chosen side hustle idea, setting you on a path toward financial independence and Side Hustle Millionaire status.

Niche Selection for Success

Once you've generated a list of potential side hustle ideas through brainstorming, the next crucial step is selecting the right niche for success. Niche selection is pivotal to building a profitable and sustainable side hustle. Here's how to navigate this critical decision-making process:

Understand the Concept of a Niche

A niche refers to a specific segment or subcategory within a broader market. It's a specialized area that caters to a particular audience with distinct needs and preferences. In the context of side hustles, choosing a niche means narrowing down your focus to a specific group of customers or a particular industry.

Why Niche Selection Matters

Niche selection plays a pivotal role in the success of your side hustle for several reasons:

- Reduced Competition: In a niche, you're likely to face less competition compared to broader markets. This can make it easier to establish your presence and capture a dedicated customer base.

- Targeted Audience: When you choose a niche, you're addressing a specific audience with known characteristics and needs. This allows you to tailor your products, services, and marketing efforts precisely to their preferences.

- Expertise and Authority: Specializing in a niche positions you as an expert or authority in that field. Customers are more likely to trust and choose businesses that demonstrate deep knowledge and understanding of their niche.

- Profit Potential: Niches often offer higher profit potential because you can charge premium prices for specialized products or services. Customers are willing to pay more for offerings that cater specifically to their needs.

How to Select the Right Niche

Choosing the right niche for your side hustle requires careful consideration and research. Here's a step-by-step guide to help you make an informed decision:

- Evaluate Your Interests and Skills: Start by assessing your own interests, passions, and skills. Consider what you enjoy doing and what you excel at. Your side hustle should align with these factors to maintain your motivation and expertise.
- Market Research: Conduct thorough market research to identify potential niches. Look for niches that have demand but aren't oversaturated. Use online tools like Google Trends, keyword research, and industry-specific forums to gather insights.

- Competitor Analysis: Study your potential competitors within your chosen niches. Analyze their strengths and weaknesses. Identify gaps in their offerings or areas where you can provide a unique value proposition.

- Target Audience: Define your target audience within the niche. Understand their demographics, preferences, pain points, and buying behaviors. Your side hustle should aim to solve their specific problems or fulfill their needs.

- Monetization Strategy: Consider how you plan to make money within the niche. Will you offer products, services, digital content, or a combination of these? Evaluate the profitability of your chosen monetization strategy.

- Passion and Longevity: Ensure that your selected niche is something you're passionate about and can see yourself committing to for the long term. Sustainable success often requires dedication and persistence.

- Scalability: Assess whether your chosen niche offers opportunities for growth and scalability. Can you expand your offerings or reach a larger audience over time?

- Feedback: Seek feedback from trusted individuals, mentors, or potential customers. Share your niche ideas and gather insights to refine your decision.

Examples of Profitable Niches

While the right niche for your side hustle will depend on your unique skills and interests, here are some examples of profitable niches that have seen success:

- Health and Wellness: Niches within the health and wellness industry, such as fitness coaching, healthy meal planning, or mental health support, have high demand.

- Technology and Gadgets: Niches related to technology, such as smartphone accessories, smart home solutions, or tech tutorials, are continually evolving and offer growth potential.

- Eco-Friendly Products: With the increasing focus on sustainability, niches like eco-friendly products, zero waste living, or renewable energy solutions are gaining traction.

- Online Learning: Educational niches, particularly in online learning and skill development, have witnessed significant growth in recent years.

- E-commerce: Niches within e-commerce, such as niche-specific apparel, unique handmade products, or curated subscription boxes, can be profitable if well-executed.

Remember that the ideal niche for your side hustle should align with your passions, skills, and long-term goals. It's not just about finding a niche that's profitable; it's about finding one that you're genuinely excited about and willing to invest time and effort into. Once you've selected the right niche, you can move forward with planning and launching your side hustle with confidence.

Chapter 3: Planning Your Side Hustle

Planning is a crucial phase of your side hustle journey, as it's where your idea begins to take shape and transform into a tangible venture. Effective planning sets the foundation for success and minimizes the risks associated with starting a new business or project. Here's a step-by-step guide to help you plan your side hustle:

Creating a Business Plan

A well-crafted business plan is the blueprint for your side hustle's success. It not only guides your actions but also serves as a tool to attract investors or secure financing if needed. Here's a comprehensive guide on how to create a business plan for your side hustle:

1. Executive Summary

The executive summary is a concise overview of your entire business plan. It should include:

- A brief description of your side hustle.

- Your mission and vision statements.
- A summary of your goals and objectives.
- A snapshot of your financial projections.
- A request for funding (if applicable).
- The executive summary should provide a clear understanding of your side hustle's purpose and potential.

2. Company Description

In this section, delve deeper into the specifics of your side hustle. Describe:

- Your business's legal structure (e.g., sole proprietorship, LLC, corporation).
- The history of your side hustle (if applicable).
- Your mission and vision statements in more detail.
- The problem your side hustle solves or the need it fulfills.
- The target market you aim to serve.

3. Market Research

Show that you've done your homework by presenting thorough market research:

- Define your target audience in detail, including demographics, behaviors, and preferences.
- Analyze your competitors, their strengths, weaknesses, and market positioning.
- Explain your unique selling proposition (USP) and how it distinguishes you from competitors.
- Provide data on market size, growth trends, and potential opportunities.

4. Products or Services

Clearly outline the products or services you plan to offer:

- Describe each offering in detail, including features, benefits, and pricing.
- Explain how your products or services address customer needs or problems.

- Highlight any intellectual property, patents, or proprietary technology related to your offerings.

5. Marketing and Sales Strategy

Detail how you'll attract and retain customers:

- Outline your marketing and promotional strategies, including online and offline tactics.
- Define your sales channels (e.g., e-commerce, direct sales, partnerships).
- Include a sales forecast, breaking down expected revenue by product, customer segment, and time period.

6. Operational Plan

Explain how your side hustle will operate on a day-to-day basis:

- Describe your location (if applicable) and any physical resources needed.

- Detail the supply chain, including suppliers and inventory management.
- Provide information on production processes, if relevant.
- Outline your staffing needs and organizational structure.

7. Financial Plan

This section is crucial for both you and potential investors:

- Create detailed financial projections, including income statements, cash flow statements, and balance sheets.
- Estimate startup costs and initial funding requirements.
- Explain your pricing strategy and revenue model.
- Project your financial performance over the next three to five years.

8. Funding Request (if applicable)

- If you're seeking external funding, specify the amount you need and how you plan to use it:
- Describe the type of funding you're seeking (e.g., equity investment, loan).
- Provide a breakdown of how you'll allocate the funds (e.g., marketing, equipment, working capital).
- Explain the expected return on investment (ROI) for investors or lenders.

9. Management and Team

Highlight your qualifications and the qualifications of key team members:

- Provide brief bios and relevant experience for yourself and any co-founders or key team members.
- Highlight key advisors, mentors, or consultants who support your side hustle.
- Describe roles and responsibilities within the organization.

10. Appendices

Include any additional information that supports your business plan:

- Market research data, surveys, or studies.
- Resumes of team members or advisors.
- Legal documents such as patents, trademarks, or contracts.
- Any other relevant documentation.

11. Review and Refine

Before finalizing your business plan, review it carefully for clarity, coherence, and accuracy. Seek feedback from trusted mentors or peers to identify any weaknesses or areas for improvement. Your business plan should be a dynamic document that adapts as your side hustle evolves.

Remember that a well-prepared business plan not only helps you navigate the challenges of starting and running a side hustle but also demonstrates your commitment and vision to potential partners, investors, or lenders. It serves as a roadmap for your entrepreneurial journey, helping you stay focused on your goals and increase the likelihood of achieving Side Hustle Millionaire status.

Setting Realistic Goals

Goals are the compass that guides your journey towards financial success and Side Hustle Millionaire status. While it's essential to dream big and aim high, setting realistic goals is equally crucial. Realistic goals are achievable, motivating, and provide a clear path to measure your progress. Here's how to set realistic goals for your side hustle:

1. Define Your Vision

Start by envisioning your desired outcome. What does financial success mean to you? What does your life look like when you achieve your goals? Define your vision in specific terms. For example, your vision might be to have a side hustle that generates $100,000 in annual revenue within five years while allowing you to maintain a work-life balance.

2. Break Down the Goals

Large, long-term goals can be overwhelming. To make them more manageable and achievable, break them down into smaller, actionable steps. These intermediate goals serve as milestones along your journey. Using the previous example, you might set intermediate goals of reaching $10,000 in revenue in the first year, $25,000 in the second year, and so on.

3. Make Them Specific and Measurable

Vague goals are challenging to track and achieve. Make your goals specific and measurable. Instead of saying, "I want to earn more money," specify, "I aim to increase my side hustle income by 20% this year." Measuring progress against concrete numbers keeps you accountable.

4. Ensure Relevance

Your goals should align with your overall vision and values. Ask yourself why each goal matters to you. If a goal doesn't contribute to your vision or fulfillment, reconsider its relevance. Keep your goals focused on what truly matters to you.

5. Set a Timeline

Establish deadlines for achieving your goals. Without a timeframe, goals can languish indefinitely. Setting deadlines creates a sense of urgency and helps you prioritize tasks. However, be realistic about the time needed to achieve each goal.

6. Consider Resources and Constraints

Take stock of the resources available to you, including time, money, and skills. Your goals should be attainable given your current circumstances. Consider any constraints that may affect your progress, such as a full-time job or limited startup capital.

7. Research and Benchmark

Research industry standards and benchmarks to ensure your goals are attainable. Understand what's realistic in your niche or market. Benchmarking can help you set goals that are both challenging and feasible.

8. Embrace Flexibility

Life is unpredictable, and your side hustle journey will have its ups and downs. Be prepared to adapt your goals when circumstances change. Flexibility doesn't mean giving up on your vision but rather adjusting your approach as needed.

9. Seek Accountability

Share your goals with someone you trust, such as a mentor, friend, or family member. Accountability can provide motivation and support. Regularly discuss your progress and setbacks with your accountability partner.

10. Celebrate Milestones

Celebrate your achievements, no matter how small. Recognizing your progress reinforces your commitment and motivates you to continue. Each milestone reached brings you one step closer to your ultimate goal.

11. Learn and Adjust

As you work toward your goals, you'll encounter challenges and learn valuable lessons. Embrace setbacks as opportunities for growth. Adjust your strategies when necessary, but don't lose sight of your vision.

12. Stay Committed

Setting realistic goals is just the beginning. Staying committed to your goals requires consistency and determination. Remind yourself regularly of your vision and the reasons you embarked on your side hustle journey.

Remember that realistic goals are not limitations but stepping stones towards your larger aspirations. They provide a roadmap to follow and allow you to measure your progress along the way. By setting realistic goals for your side hustle, you'll be well-equipped to navigate the challenges and uncertainties of entrepreneurship while steadily moving closer to your vision of financial success and Side Hustle Millionaire status.

Chapter 4: Building Your Brand

Your brand is more than just a logo or a name; it's the essence of your side hustle. Building a strong brand is essential for attracting customers, fostering trust, and achieving long-term success. Here's how to effectively build your brand:

Crafting Your Unique Selling Proposition (USP)

In a crowded marketplace, having a Unique Selling Proposition (USP) is the secret sauce that sets your side hustle apart from the competition. Your USP defines what makes your business unique and why customers should choose you over others. Crafting a compelling USP is essential for attracting and retaining customers. Here's how to create an effective USP:

1. Understand Your Target Audience

Before crafting your USP, you must understand your target audience inside and out. Dive deep into their needs, preferences, pain points, and desires. What problems are they trying to solve? What motivates them to make a purchase? The more you know about your audience, the better you can tailor your USP to resonate with them.

2. Identify Your Unique Qualities

What makes your side hustle distinct? Consider your strengths, attributes, and offerings. Are you the fastest, the most affordable, the most innovative, or the most customer-centric? Think about your:

Expertise: Do you possess unique knowledge or skills that set you apart?

Process: Is there a proprietary process or methodology you use?

Products or Services: Do you offer something that no one else does?

Values: Are your values and mission aligned with your customers' values?

3. Analyze Your Competitors

Research your competitors to identify gaps or opportunities in the market. What are they doing well, and where do they fall short? A strong USP often addresses a need or pain point that your competitors haven't fully tapped into. Look for areas where you can provide a better solution or a different approach.

4. Solve a Problem or Fulfill a Need

A powerful USP should focus on solving a specific problem or fulfilling a distinct need for your target audience. Clearly articulate how your side hustle addresses this issue and provides value. Highlight the benefits customers will gain from choosing your business.

5. Keep It Simple and Clear

Your USP should be concise and easy to understand. Avoid jargon or overly complex language. Use simple, straightforward messaging that immediately communicates your unique value. A strong USP can often be expressed in a single sentence.

6. Emphasize Benefits, Not Features

While features are important, customers are primarily interested in how a product or service benefits them. Describe the outcomes, advantages, and transformations that customers can expect. Emphasize the "what's in it for me" aspect to make your USP compelling.

7. Test Your USP

Before finalizing your USP, test it with a sample audience or potential customers. Gather feedback to ensure it resonates and is clearly understood. Adjust your USP based on their input to make it even more impactful.

8. Communicate Your USP Consistently

Once you've crafted your USP, integrate it into all your marketing materials and communication channels. Consistency is key in reinforcing your brand's unique qualities. Use it in your website copy, social media profiles, advertising campaigns, and customer interactions.

9. Highlight It in Your Elevator Pitch

Your USP should be an integral part of your elevator pitch, a brief and compelling summary of your business. When you have a concise, impactful USP, it becomes a central element of how you introduce your side hustle to others.

10. Evolve Your USP as Needed

As your business grows and evolves, your USP may need adjustments. Market conditions, customer preferences, and industry trends change over time. Regularly assess your USP to ensure it remains relevant and resonates with your target audience.

A well-crafted USP not only attracts customers but also helps you build brand loyalty and customer advocacy. It communicates your unique value and sets expectations for what customers can experience when they choose your side hustle. By investing time and thought into creating a compelling USP, you'll differentiate your business in the marketplace and move closer to achieving Side Hustle Millionaire status.

Branding and Marketing Strategies

In the world of side hustles, effective branding and marketing strategies are the engines that drive visibility, customer engagement, and revenue growth. Whether you're just starting or looking to elevate your existing side hustle, here's a comprehensive guide to help you create and implement successful branding and marketing strategies:

Branding Strategies

- Define Your Brand Identity: Start by defining your brand's core identity, including your mission, values, and unique selling proposition (USP). A strong brand identity serves as the foundation for all your branding efforts

- Create a Memorable Logo and Visual Elements: Invest in professional logo design and choose a color palette and typography that align with your brand's personality.

These visual elements should be consistent across all touchpoints.

- Develop a Distinctive Voice: Establish a brand voice that reflects your values and resonates with your target audience. Consistency in your brand's tone and messaging helps build recognition and trust.

- Tell Your Brand Story: Share your journey, experiences, and values through storytelling. Authentic and relatable narratives humanize your brand and create emotional connections with customers.

- Prioritize Consistency: Ensure consistency in your branding elements, from your website and social media profiles to marketing materials and packaging. This consistency builds brand recognition.

Online Presence

- Professional Website: Your website is often the first point of contact for potential customers. Invest in a professional, user-friendly website that reflects your brand identity and offers a seamless user experience.

- Social Media Engagement: Choose the social media platforms most relevant to your target audience and engage consistently. Share valuable content, interact with followers, and use social media to showcase your brand's personality.

- Content Marketing: Develop a content marketing strategy that provides value to your audience. Create blog posts, videos, podcasts, or other content that educates, entertains, or inspires. Content helps establish your expertise and authority.

- Email Marketing: Build and nurture an email list to stay connected with your audience. Send regular newsletters, promotions, or updates to keep customers engaged and informed about your side hustle.

Marketing Strategies

- Understand Your Target Audience: Continuously refine your understanding of your target audience. Conduct market research, gather customer feedback, and adapt your strategies to meet their evolving needs.

- Search Engine Optimization (SEO): Optimize your online content for search engines to improve visibility in search results. Use relevant keywords and create high-quality, shareable content.

- Paid Advertising: Consider using paid advertising on platforms like Google Ads or social media ads to reach a larger audience. Target ads based on demographics, interests, and behavior to maximize ROI.

- Influencer Marketing: Collaborate with influencers in your niche to promote your side hustle. Influencers can help you reach a broader and more engaged audience.

- Referral and Affiliate Programs: Encourage satisfied customers to refer others to your side hustle by offering referral incentives. Create affiliate programs to incentivize partners to promote your products or services.

- Public Relations: Build relationships with media outlets, bloggers, and industry influencers. Press coverage and mentions can boost your brand's credibility and visibility.

Customer Relationship Management

- Outstanding Customer Service: Provide exceptional customer service to build trust and loyalty. Address inquiries and resolve issues promptly and professionally.

- Feedback and Reviews: Encourage customers to leave reviews and provide feedback. Positive reviews serve as social proof and can influence potential customers.

- Engagement and Community Building: Create an online community around your brand. Engage with customers on social media, host webinars or workshops, and create a sense of belonging among your audience.

Measuring and Adjusting

- Track Key Metrics: Use analytics tools to monitor the performance of your branding and marketing efforts. Measure website traffic, conversion rates, social media engagement, and other relevant metrics.
- A/B Testing: Experiment with different strategies and tactics through A/B testing. This allows you to refine your approach based on data-driven insights.
- Adapt to Market Changes: Stay informed about industry trends and shifts in customer behavior. Be ready to adapt your branding and marketing strategies to remain competitive.

Successful branding and marketing strategies require ongoing effort, adaptability, and a deep understanding of your audience. By consistently delivering value, building brand recognition, and engaging with customers, you can position your side hustle for sustained growth and success.

Chapter 5: Financial Management

Effective financial management is at the core of turning your side hustle into a profitable venture and achieving your goal of reaching Side Hustle Millionaire status. Here's a concise guide to help you manage your side hustle's finances:

Budgeting and Savings Strategies

Budgeting and saving are the cornerstones of financial success, and they play a critical role in achieving your goal of reaching Side Hustle Millionaire status. Proper budgeting allows you to manage your income, control expenses, and allocate funds strategically, while saving helps you build wealth and secure your financial future. Here's a comprehensive guide to effective budgeting and savings strategies for your side hustle:

Budgeting Strategies

- Create a Detailed Budget: Start by listing all your sources of income, including your side hustle earnings, and then categorize your expenses. Divide them into fixed expenses (e.g., rent, utilities) and variable expenses (e.g., groceries, entertainment). A detailed budget provides a clear picture of your financial situation.

- Set Clear Financial Goals: Define specific financial goals, both short-term and long-term. For example, set a goal to save a certain percentage of your side hustle income each month, pay off debt, or invest in business growth.

- Prioritize Essentials: Ensure that your budget covers essential expenses first, such as housing, utilities, groceries, and debt payments. These are the non-negotiables that must be accounted for.

- Control Discretionary Spending: Be mindful of discretionary spending on non-essential items like dining out, entertainment, or impulse purchases. Allocate a reasonable amount for these expenses within your budget.

- Emergency Fund: Include contributions to an emergency fund in your budget. Aim to save at least three to six months' worth of living expenses in case of unexpected financial challenges.

- Track and Review Regularly: Monitor your spending regularly and compare it to your budget. Use budgeting tools or apps to help you stay on track. Review your budget monthly to make necessary adjustments.

- Debt Repayment Plan: If you have outstanding debts, develop a plan for paying them off systematically. Focus on high-interest debts first to minimize interest expenses.

Savings Strategies

- Pay Yourself First: Treat your savings as a non-negotiable expense. Automate transfers from your side hustle income into savings accounts. By paying yourself first, you ensure that saving becomes a consistent habit.

- Create Specific Savings Goals: Set clear and achievable savings goals, such as saving for retirement, a down payment on a home, or a dream vacation. Knowing what you're saving for can motivate you to stay disciplined.

- Emergency Fund: Prioritize building an emergency fund to cover unexpected expenses without derailing your budget. Start with a small, manageable goal and gradually increase it over time.

- Use Tax-Advantaged Accounts: Take advantage of tax-advantaged savings accounts like Individual Retirement Accounts (IRAs) and 401(k)s. These accounts offer tax benefits and can help you grow your savings more efficiently.

- Automate Savings: Set up automatic transfers to your savings accounts on a regular basis. Treating savings like a bill ensures that you consistently contribute to your financial future.

- Invest Wisely: Once you've built an emergency fund and paid off high-interest debt, consider investing your savings in diversified portfolios or assets that have the potential to grow over time. Consult a financial advisor for guidance.

- Reinvest in Your Side Hustle: Allocate a portion of your savings to reinvest in your side hustle. This can include upgrading equipment, expanding your product line, or investing in marketing efforts to grow your income.

- Review and Adjust: Regularly review your savings goals and progress. Adjust your savings strategies as your financial situation changes or when you achieve specific milestones.

- Lifestyle Inflation: Be cautious about letting your lifestyle inflate as your side hustle income grows. Instead of increasing your spending in proportion to your earnings, continue to prioritize saving and investing.

- Seek Professional Advice: If you're unsure about the best savings and investment strategies for your side hustle income, consider consulting a financial advisor. They can provide tailored guidance based on your goals and risk tolerance.

Effective budgeting and savings strategies are essential for building financial security, achieving your financial goals, and ultimately attaining Side Hustle Millionaire status. By consistently applying these principles, you'll not only enjoy the benefits of your side hustle but also secure a prosperous future.

Pricing Your Products or Services

Determining the right pricing strategy for your products or services is a crucial aspect of running a successful side hustle. Your pricing not only affects your profitability but also plays a significant role in attracting customers and achieving your financial goals. Here's a comprehensive guide to help you navigate the process of pricing effectively:

1. Know Your Costs

Before setting a price, it's essential to understand your costs. Calculate all expenses associated with producing or delivering your products or services. This includes raw materials, labor, overhead, and any fixed or variable costs. Knowing your costs ensures that you cover expenses and generate a profit.

2. Research the Market

Study your competitors and the broader market to gain insights into pricing trends and customer expectations. Analyze what similar products or services are priced at and identify any gaps or opportunities. This research helps you position your offerings competitively.

3. Consider Value-Based Pricing

Value-based pricing involves setting prices based on the perceived value your product or service provides to customers. Focus on the benefits and outcomes your customers receive. If your offering solves a significant problem or fulfills a need, you may justify a higher price.

4. Understand Your Target Audience

Different customer segments may have varying price sensitivity. Consider the demographics, preferences, and purchasing behavior of your target audience when setting prices. Price discrimination, such as offering tiered pricing for different customer groups, can be an effective strategy.

5. Factor in Profit Margin

Determine the profit margin you aim to achieve. Your profit margin reflects the percentage of revenue that represents profit after covering costs. Consider how your pricing strategy aligns with your profit goals and long-term financial objectives.

6. Offer Multiple Price Points

Provide customers with options by offering multiple price points or packages. This strategy appeals to a broader range of customers. For example, you can offer a basic, standard, and premium version of your product or service with varying features and prices.

7. Consider Bundling

Bundling involves packaging multiple products or services together at a discounted price. This strategy can increase the overall value perceived by customers and incentivize them to make a larger purchase.

8. Monitor and Adjust

Pricing is not static; it requires continuous monitoring and adjustment. Keep an eye on your competitors, market trends, and customer feedback. Be willing to adjust your prices if necessary to remain competitive or meet changing customer expectations.

9. Test Your Pricing

Experiment with different pricing strategies to determine what works best for your side hustle. A/B testing, where you offer different price points to segments of your audience, can provide valuable insights into which pricing strategy is most effective.

10. Be Transparent

Open and transparent pricing builds trust with your customers. Clearly communicate what customers get for their money and avoid hidden fees or unexpected charges.

11. Factor in Taxes and Fees

Consider taxes and fees that may affect your pricing. Sales tax, transaction fees, and payment processing fees can impact your revenue and profitability. Ensure that your pricing accounts for these expenses.

12. Offer Discounts and Promotions

Strategically use discounts, promotions, and limited-time offers to attract customers and boost sales. Be cautious not to devalue your products or services with excessive discounts.

13. Leverage Psychological Pricing

Psychological pricing techniques, such as using prices ending in "9" (e.g., $19.99), can influence purchasing behavior. Experiment with these pricing strategies to see how they affect customer response.

14. Monitor Customer Acquisition Costs

Consider the cost of acquiring each customer when setting prices. If your customer acquisition costs are high, you may need to price your products or services accordingly to ensure profitability.

15. Educate Customers

Help customers understand the value they receive for the price. Use persuasive marketing and communication strategies to showcase the benefits and advantages of choosing your offerings.

16. Seek Customer Feedback

Regularly gather feedback from customers about your pricing. Understand their perception of value and whether they find your prices fair. Customer input can guide adjustments to your pricing strategy.

Effective pricing is a balancing act that requires careful consideration of costs, competition, and customer perceptions. By implementing a well-thought-out pricing strategy, you can maximize revenue, build customer loyalty, and work toward achieving Side Hustle Millionaire status while providing value to your customers.

Chapter 6: Launching Your Side Hustle

Launching your side hustle is an exciting and pivotal moment on your journey to financial success and Side Hustle Millionaire status. Here's a concise guide to help you navigate the process of launching your side hustle successfully:

Building an Online Presence

In today's digital age, establishing a strong online presence is essential for the success of your side hustle. An effective online presence not only helps you reach a wider audience but also builds credibility and trust with potential customers. Here's a comprehensive guide to building and optimizing your online presence:

1. Create a Professional Website

Your website serves as the digital storefront for your side hustle. It should be well-designed, easy to navigate, and optimized for both desktop and mobile devices. Include essential information about your products or services, contact details, and a clear call to action.

2. Choose the Right Domain Name

Select a domain name that reflects your brand and is easy to remember. Keep it concise and avoid using special characters or hyphens. Ensure that the domain is available and purchase it from a reputable registrar.

3. Optimize for Search Engines (SEO)

Implement search engine optimization (SEO) best practices to improve your website's visibility in search engine results. Conduct keyword research to identify relevant keywords, optimize your content, and use meta tags and descriptions. Regularly update your website with fresh, valuable content.

4. Engage in Content Marketing

Create and share high-quality, relevant content that resonates with your target audience. Content can include blog posts, articles, videos, podcasts, infographics, and more. Content marketing helps establish your expertise and attracts organic traffic to your website.

5. Utilize Social Media

Identify the social media platforms where your target audience is most active, and establish a presence on those platforms. Regularly post engaging content, interact with your followers, and use social media advertising to expand your reach.

6. Email Marketing

Build an email list and use email marketing campaigns to stay connected with your audience. Send newsletters, promotions, and updates to keep customers engaged and informed about your side hustle.

7. Implement E-commerce Solutions

If you sell products online, consider setting up an e-commerce platform on your website. Ensure a smooth and secure shopping experience for customers, and offer various payment options.

8. Use Online Advertising

Invest in online advertising to reach a broader audience. Platforms like Google Ads and social media advertising allow you to target specific demographics, interests, and behaviors. Monitor your ad campaigns and adjust them for optimal results.

9. Create Visual Content

Visual content, such as images, videos, and infographics, is highly shareable and engaging. Use visuals to convey your brand message and showcase your products or services.

10. Leverage Online Reviews and Testimonials

Encourage satisfied customers to leave reviews and testimonials on platforms like Google My Business, Yelp, or your website. Positive reviews build trust and credibility with potential customers.

11. Build Backlinks

Backlinks from reputable websites can improve your website's authority and SEO ranking. Network with other businesses, guest post on industry-related blogs, and engage in content partnerships to build backlinks.

12. Monitor and Analyze

Use web analytics tools to track the performance of your online presence. Measure website traffic, conversion rates, social media engagement, and other relevant metrics. Analyze the data to make informed decisions and refine your online strategies.

13. Stay Consistent

Consistency is key to maintaining a strong online presence. Regularly update your website and social media profiles, respond to customer inquiries promptly, and consistently deliver valuable content.

14. Protect Your Online Reputation

Monitor what people are saying about your side hustle online. Address negative feedback professionally and use it as an opportunity to improve. Cultivate a positive online reputation to build trust.

15. Adapt to Trends

Stay informed about industry trends and emerging technologies. Be ready to adapt your online presence strategies to leverage new opportunities and remain competitive.

Building and maintaining a robust online presence is an ongoing effort that requires dedication and adaptability. By implementing these strategies and staying committed to your online marketing efforts, you can effectively reach your target audience, build brand recognition, and ultimately achieve success with your side hustle.

Getting Your First Customers

Securing your first customers is a significant milestone for any side hustle. It's a critical step toward generating revenue and validating your business concept. However, it can be a challenging process, especially when you're just starting. Here's a comprehensive guide to help you acquire your first customers effectively:

1. Define Your Ideal Customer

Before you can attract customers, you need to know who your ideal customer is. Create detailed customer personas that outline demographics, preferences, pain points, and buying behavior. Understanding your target audience is key to tailoring your marketing efforts effectively.

2. Build a Professional Online Presence

A professional online presence is crucial in today's digital world. Create a professional website, establish social media profiles, and optimize them for search engines. Ensure that your online presence reflects your brand and offerings.

3. Leverage Your Network

Start by reaching out to your existing network of friends, family, and colleagues. They can serve as your initial customers or refer potential clients to you. Word-of-mouth referrals are powerful in the early stages of your side hustle.

4. Offer a Compelling Value Proposition

Clearly communicate the value your products or services provide to customers. Highlight how you solve their problems, fulfill their needs, or enhance their lives. A strong value proposition makes it easier to attract and retain customers.

5. Offer Special Promotions

Consider offering special promotions or discounts to incentivize early adoption. Limited-time offers or introductory pricing can encourage potential customers to make their first purchase.

6. Utilize Social Media

Engage with your target audience on social media platforms where they are most active. Share valuable content, interact with followers, and use social media advertising to expand your reach.

7. Attend Local Events and Networking

Participate in local events, trade shows, or networking meetings relevant to your industry. These gatherings provide opportunities to connect with potential customers and other businesses in your niche.

8. Collaborate with Influencers

Collaborating with influencers in your niche can help you gain credibility and reach a wider audience. Influencers can promote your products or services to their followers, generating interest and potential sales.

9. Offer Exceptional Customer Service

Provide outstanding customer service from the beginning. Happy customers are more likely to become repeat buyers and refer others to your side hustle.

10. Collect and Showcase Testimonials

Gather testimonials and reviews from satisfied customers and display them prominently on your website and marketing materials. Positive feedback builds trust with potential customers.

11. Join Online Communities

Participate in online communities and forums related to your industry. Share your expertise, answer questions, and establish yourself as a knowledgeable and trustworthy resource.

12. Create Valuable Content

Develop high-quality content that educates, entertains, or solves problems for your target audience. Content marketing through blog posts, videos, podcasts, or infographics can help attract organic traffic to your website.

13. Engage in Email Marketing

Build an email list and send regular newsletters, promotions, or updates to stay connected with potential customers. Email marketing is a powerful tool for nurturing leads and converting them into paying customers.

14. Offer Exceptional Value

Go the extra mile to provide exceptional value in your products or services. Delight your customers with quality, reliability, and a positive experience. Satisfied customers are more likely to become brand advocates.

15. Be Patient and Persistent

Getting your first customers may take time, so be patient and persistent. Keep refining your approach based on customer feedback and market insights. Stay committed to your goals and adapt as needed.

16. Analyze and Adjust

Regularly analyze your customer acquisition strategies and their effectiveness. Use data and customer feedback to make informed adjustments to your marketing efforts.

Securing your first customers is a pivotal moment in your side hustle journey. It's a testament to your hard work and dedication. By implementing these strategies and staying focused on providing value to your customers, you can not only attract your first customers but also lay a solid foundation for your side hustle's growth and success.

Chapter 7: Scaling Up for Success

Scaling up your side hustle is a thrilling and ambitious endeavor that involves taking your business to the next level of growth and profitability. Whether you're a solopreneur or a small team, the dream of reaching Side Hustle Millionaire status is within reach. However, scaling up requires careful planning, strategic decisions, and a commitment to excellence.

In this chapter, we'll explore the essential steps and considerations for scaling up your side hustle effectively. We'll delve into areas such as expanding your customer base, increasing revenue streams, optimizing operations, and maintaining financial stability. Scaling up is not just about growing in size; it's about achieving sustainable success that aligns with your long-term goals.

Whether you're looking to transform your side hustle into a full-time venture or expand your reach and impact, the principles of scaling up remain the same. We'll provide actionable insights, best practices, and strategies that can help you navigate the challenges and opportunities that come with growth.

Scaling up can be a transformative journey that requires adaptability, resilience, and a forward-thinking mindset. It's about maximizing the potential of your side hustle, pushing boundaries, and turning your vision into reality. As you embark on this exciting path, remember that success is not only measured by financial achievements but also by the positive impact you create for your customers and the fulfillment you derive from pursuing your passion.

So, let's dive into the world of scaling up for success, where you'll learn how to expand your side hustle while maintaining the core values and principles that make your venture unique. Whether you're just starting to contemplate growth or you're already on your way, this chapter will provide valuable insights to help you achieve your goals and become a Side Hustle Millionaire.

Time Management and Scaling Tips

As you embark on the journey of scaling up your side hustle, effective time management becomes even more critical. Balancing growth initiatives with your existing workload requires careful planning and prioritization. Here are essential time management and scaling tips to help you navigate this challenging but rewarding phase:

1. Set Clear Goals

Begin by defining clear and specific goals for your scaling efforts. Whether it's doubling your customer base, increasing revenue by a certain percentage, or expanding your product line, having well-defined objectives provides direction and motivation.

2. Prioritize Tasks

Identify the most critical tasks that contribute directly to your scaling goals. Prioritize these tasks and focus your time and energy on them. Use techniques like the Eisenhower Matrix to categorize tasks into four quadrants: urgent and important, important but not urgent, urgent but not important, and neither urgent nor important.

3. Delegate and Outsource

Recognize that you can't do everything on your own. Delegate tasks that don't require your expertise or are time-consuming to trusted team members or freelancers. Outsourcing certain aspects of your business can free up valuable time for strategic efforts.

4. Time Blocking

Implement time blocking to structure your workday effectively. Dedicate specific blocks of time to particular tasks or categories of work. This helps you stay organized and ensures that important activities don't get sidelined by distractions.

5. Automate Routine Tasks

Identify routine and repetitive tasks that can be automated. Use tools and software to streamline processes like email marketing, social media scheduling, and customer support. Automation saves time and reduces the risk of errors.

6. Focus on High-Value Activities

As the leader of your side hustle, your time is most valuable when spent on high-impact activities. This may include strategic planning, business development, relationship building, and decision-making. Delegate or automate low-value tasks to free up your schedule.

7. Time Audit

Conduct a time audit to analyze how you're currently spending your time. Track your activities for a week or two to identify time-wasting habits and areas where you can make improvements.

8. Limit Distractions

Minimize distractions by creating a dedicated workspace, turning off non-essential notifications, and setting boundaries with family and friends during work hours. Consider using productivity apps or website blockers to stay focused.

9. Batch Similar Tasks

Group similar tasks together and tackle them during dedicated time blocks. For instance, handle all your email correspondence at specific times rather than checking it constantly throughout the day. Batching tasks reduces context-switching and improves efficiency.

10. Regularly Review and Adjust

Frequently review your time management strategies to assess their effectiveness. Be willing to adjust your approach based on what's working and what isn't. Continual improvement is key to optimizing your time.

11. Invest in Personal Development

Enhance your time management skills through personal development. Read books, take courses, or seek advice from successful entrepreneurs who have scaled their businesses. Learning time management techniques can be a game-changer.

12. Stay Healthy and Rested

Don't neglect your physical and mental well-being. Proper nutrition, regular exercise, and sufficient sleep contribute to your overall productivity and decision-making abilities. A healthy body and mind are crucial for effective time management.

13. Plan for Scalability

As you scale, consider the scalability of your processes and systems. Invest in technology and infrastructure that can grow with your business. Plan for future growth to avoid bottlenecks and disruptions.

14. Be Realistic

While ambition is commendable, be realistic about what you can achieve within a given timeframe. Scaling takes time and effort, and rushing the process can lead to burnout. Set achievable milestones and adjust your expectations as needed.

15. Celebrate Achievements

Acknowledge and celebrate your scaling milestones. Recognizing your accomplishments motivates you to keep pushing forward and reminds you of the progress you've made.

Effective time management is the linchpin of scaling your side hustle successfully. By setting clear goals, prioritizing tasks, and implementing these tips, you'll not only manage your time more efficiently but also increase your chances of achieving Side Hustle Millionaire status. Remember that scaling is a journey, and mastering time management is a valuable skill that will serve you well in the long run.

Expanding Your Business

Scaling up your side hustle often involves expanding your business to reach new markets, attract more customers, and increase your revenue. It's an exciting phase that comes with opportunities and challenges. Here's a comprehensive guide to help you navigate the process of expanding your business successfully:

1. Market Research

Before expanding, conduct thorough market research to identify new opportunities and assess demand. Understand the needs and preferences of your target audience in the new market. Analyze competition, local regulations, and cultural factors that may affect your expansion.

2. Create a Growth Plan

Develop a comprehensive growth plan that outlines your expansion strategy, goals, and timelines. Define the resources and investments required, including finances, personnel, and technology. A well-structured plan provides a roadmap for your expansion efforts.

3. Financial Preparation

Ensure your finances are in order before expanding. Assess the capital required for the expansion and secure funding if necessary. Evaluate your existing cash flow and profitability to determine if you can support the growth without compromising your financial stability.

4. Product or Service Adaptation

Tailor your products or services to meet the specific needs of the new market. This may involve adjustments in pricing, features, branding, or packaging. Ensure that your offerings resonate with the local audience.

5. Legal and Regulatory Compliance

Understand the legal and regulatory requirements of the new market. This includes business registration, licenses, permits, tax obligations, and compliance with local laws. Consult legal experts to ensure full compliance.

6. Marketing and Promotion

Develop a targeted marketing and promotion strategy to introduce your business to the new market. This may involve localized advertising campaigns, social media efforts, partnerships with local influencers, and attending industry-specific events.

7. Distribution and Logistics

Consider how you will deliver your products or services to customers in the new market. Establish efficient distribution channels and logistics networks. Ensure that you can meet demand without compromising on quality or delivery times.

8. Team and Talent

Assess your team's capabilities and determine if you need to expand your workforce. Hire local talent who understand the market and can assist in the expansion process. Provide training and support to integrate them into your company culture.

9. Technology and Infrastructure

Upgrade your technology infrastructure to support the expansion. Ensure that your systems, websites, and e-commerce platforms can handle increased traffic and transactions. Invest in technology that streamlines operations and enhances customer experience.

10. Customer Support

Provide exceptional customer support in the new market to build trust and loyalty. Offer localized customer service options and channels, and be responsive to inquiries and concerns. Happy customers are more likely to become repeat buyers.

11. Monitor and Evaluate

Implement key performance indicators (KPIs) and metrics to measure the success of your expansion efforts. Continuously monitor and evaluate your performance against your goals. Be prepared to make adjustments based on data and feedback.

12. Risk Management

Identify potential risks and challenges associated with the expansion and develop mitigation strategies. Be prepared to adapt to unforeseen circumstances or market changes.

13. Build Relationships

Network and establish relationships with local businesses, organizations, and influencers in the new market. Building a strong network can open doors to opportunities and support your growth.

14. Stay Committed to Quality

Maintain the quality and consistency of your products or services throughout the expansion. Quality is a crucial factor in building a positive reputation and retaining customers.

15. Plan for Scaling Further

While your current expansion is a significant step, consider how it fits into your long-term growth plans. Plan for future scaling efforts and how each expansion aligns with your overall business strategy.

Expanding your business is a substantial undertaking that requires careful planning, commitment, and a willingness to adapt. It's an opportunity to reach new heights and achieve Side

Hustle Millionaire status. By following these steps and staying focused on your goals, you can successfully expand your business and make a meaningful impact in new markets.

Chapter 8: Managing Challenges

While the journey of scaling up your side hustle is filled with exciting possibilities and growth, it's also accompanied by its fair share of challenges. As you aim to achieve Side Hustle Millionaire status, it's essential to acknowledge and effectively manage these challenges to ensure the sustainability and success of your venture.

In this chapter, we'll explore the common challenges that entrepreneurs face when scaling their side hustles and provide actionable strategies to overcome them. From navigating financial hurdles to maintaining work-life balance and addressing operational complexities, we'll delve into the key issues that may arise during the scaling process.

Scaling a side hustle requires adaptability, resilience, and a strategic approach to problem-solving. Challenges are not roadblocks but rather opportunities for growth and learning. By understanding the challenges you may encounter and proactively addressing them, you can steer your side hustle toward continued expansion and success.

Join us as we navigate the world of managing challenges during the scaling journey, offering insights and solutions to help you overcome obstacles, stay on course, and reach your ultimate goal of becoming a Side Hustle Millionaire.

Dealing with Burnout

Burnout is a pervasive issue that affects many entrepreneurs, especially those who are scaling up their side hustles. As you strive to achieve Side Hustle Millionaire status, the demands and pressures of managing a growing business can take a toll on your physical and mental well-being. Recognizing the signs of burnout and implementing strategies to prevent and overcome it is crucial for your long-term success. Here's a comprehensive guide to help you deal with burnout effectively:

Recognizing Burnout

Physical and Emotional Exhaustion: Burnout often manifests as extreme fatigue, both physically and emotionally. You may feel drained and depleted, unable to summon the energy needed to tackle daily tasks.

- Decreased Performance: Burnout can lead to a decline in your work performance. You may find it challenging to concentrate, make decisions, or complete tasks effectively.

- Increased Cynicism: You might develop a negative and cynical attitude toward your work, clients, or colleagues. This can erode your passion and enthusiasm for your side hustle.

- Loss of Interest: Burnout can cause you to lose interest in activities you once enjoyed, including the aspects of your side hustle that used to bring you satisfaction.

- Health Problems: Chronic stress and burnout can lead to various health issues, including headaches, digestive problems, and weakened immunity.

Strategies to Prevent Burnout

- Set Boundaries: Establish clear boundaries between work and personal life. Allocate specific hours for your side hustle and prioritize downtime to relax and recharge.

- Delegate and Outsource: Recognize that you can't do everything on your own. Delegate tasks to team members or outsource responsibilities when possible to lighten your workload.

- Prioritize Self-Care: Make self-care a non-negotiable part of your routine. This includes regular exercise, healthy eating, adequate sleep, and mindfulness practices like meditation.

- Time Management: Improve your time management skills to work more efficiently and reduce stress. Use techniques like time blocking and prioritization to make the most of your day.

- Learn to Say No: Resist the urge to overcommit. Politely decline additional tasks or projects that you cannot realistically handle without sacrificing your well-being.

- Seek Support: Share your feelings and concerns with trusted friends, family members, or a therapist. Don't hesitate to ask for help or advice when needed.

- Take Breaks: Incorporate short breaks into your workday to refresh your mind. Even a few minutes of stretching or deep breathing can make a significant difference.

- Set Realistic Goals: Avoid setting overly ambitious or unrealistic goals. Break down larger objectives into smaller, achievable milestones to reduce feelings of overwhelm.

Strategies to Overcome Burnout

- Disconnect: Unplug from work-related technology and communication during your personal time. This includes turning off work email notifications and setting clear "off" hours.

- Revisit Your Why: Reconnect with your initial passion and motivation for your side hustle. Revisiting your "why" can reignite your enthusiasm and sense of purpose.

- Seek Professional Help: If burnout persists and significantly affects your well-being, consider seeking support from a mental health professional who can provide coping strategies and guidance.

- Review and Adjust Goals: Assess whether your goals are aligned with your values and priorities. Adjust your goals if necessary to create a healthier work-life balance.

- Delegate More: Continue delegating tasks and responsibilities to ensure that you're not shouldering an excessive workload.

- Schedule Regular Breaks: Incorporate regular breaks, vacations, and downtime into your schedule to prevent burnout from recurring.

Remember that burnout is not a sign of weakness but a common challenge that many entrepreneurs face. By recognizing the signs early, implementing preventive measures, and seeking help when needed, you can effectively deal with burnout and maintain the momentum on your path to achieving Side Hustle Millionaire status. Your well-being is a valuable asset on this journey, and taking care of yourself is essential for long-term success.

Overcoming Common Obstacles

As you strive to scale up your side hustle and reach Side Hustle Millionaire status, you'll inevitably encounter various obstacles along the way. These challenges are a natural part of entrepreneurship and can test your determination and resilience. To help you navigate these hurdles effectively, we'll explore some of the common obstacles faced by side hustlers and provide strategies for overcoming them.

1. Financial Constraints

One of the most common obstacles for side hustlers is limited financial resources. Balancing a full-time job with your side hustle can make it challenging to invest in growth, hire additional help, or expand operations.

Solution: Start small and bootstrap your way to success. Carefully manage your finances, reinvest profits, and explore cost-effective strategies like outsourcing, partnerships, or seeking funding when necessary.

2. Time Management

Balancing your full-time job, personal life, and side hustle can be a significant time management challenge. Finding enough hours in the day to juggle multiple responsibilities can lead to burnout.

Solution: Implement effective time management techniques, such as setting priorities, creating schedules, and delegating tasks. Focus on high-impact activities and leverage automation tools to streamline processes.

3. Customer Acquisition

Attracting and retaining customers is a common challenge for side hustlers, especially when competing with established businesses. Finding the right marketing strategies to reach your target audience can be challenging.

Solution: Invest in understanding your customers' needs and preferences. Tailor your marketing efforts to address their pain points, leverage word-of-mouth referrals, and harness the power of digital marketing and social media.

4. Burnout

The demands of a side hustle can lead to burnout, impacting your physical and mental well-being. Balancing work, family, and your business can leave you feeling overwhelmed.

Solution: Prioritize self-care, set boundaries, and practice effective stress management techniques. Seek support from friends, family, or professionals when needed.

5. Competition

Competing in a crowded market can make it difficult to stand out and gain market share.

Established competitors may have more resources and brand recognition.

Solution: Differentiate your side hustle by offering a unique value proposition, exceptional customer service, or a niche focus. Continuously innovate and adapt to stay ahead of the competition.

6. Legal and Regulatory Hurdles

Navigating the legal and regulatory requirements of running a side hustle, such as taxes, licenses, and permits, can be complex and time-consuming.

Solution: Seek legal counsel or consult experts to ensure compliance. Familiarize yourself with the specific regulations in your industry and location, and keep meticulous records to ease tax filing.

7. Scaling Challenges

Scaling your side hustle to meet growing demand presents its own set of challenges. Maintaining quality, expanding operations, and managing a larger team can be overwhelming.

Solution: Plan for scalability from the outset. Invest in systems, processes, and technology that can accommodate growth. Prioritize maintaining quality and consider phased expansion to manage growth effectively.

8. Market Changes

External factors, such as economic fluctuations or shifts in consumer behavior, can impact your side hustle's performance and profitability.

Solution: Stay adaptable and responsive to market changes. Diversify your offerings, monitor industry trends, and be prepared to pivot your business strategy when needed.

9. Work-Life Balance

Maintaining a healthy work-life balance can be a persistent challenge for side hustlers, especially when working long hours on top of a full-time job.

Solution: Set clear boundaries, communicate your needs to family and friends, and allocate dedicated downtime for relaxation and rejuvenation.

10. Self-Doubt and Fear of Failure

Entrepreneurship often comes with moments of self-doubt and fear of failure. These psychological obstacles can hinder your progress.

Solution: Develop resilience and a growth mindset. Surround yourself with a support network of like-minded individuals who can provide encouragement and perspective.

Overcoming common obstacles is an integral part of your journey to Side Hustle Millionaire status. Each challenge you encounter presents an opportunity for growth and learning. By approaching these hurdles with a proactive mindset, adaptability, and a commitment to your long-term goals, you can navigate the path to success with confidence and determination. Remember that the road to success is rarely linear, and it's your ability to overcome obstacles that sets you apart as an entrepreneur.

Chapter 9: Measuring Success

As you scale up your side hustle with the goal of achieving Side Hustle Millionaire status, it's essential to have a clear understanding of what success means to you and how to measure it. Success is a multifaceted concept that goes beyond financial achievements. It encompasses your personal fulfillment, the impact you make, and the goals you set for your side hustle.

In this chapter, we'll explore the various dimensions of measuring success in the context of your side hustle journey. We'll delve into not only the tangible metrics such as revenue, profit, and market share but also the intangible aspects like work-life balance, personal growth, and community impact.

Success is a deeply personal and subjective pursuit. What constitutes success for one side hustler may differ from another. Therefore, it's crucial to define your own version of success and set meaningful goals that align with your values and aspirations.

We'll also discuss the importance of setting realistic and achievable milestones to track your progress. By breaking down your larger goals into smaller, manageable steps, you can measure your success incrementally and stay motivated throughout your side hustle journey.

Additionally, we'll explore the significance of celebrating your achievements, no matter how small they may seem. Recognizing your successes and milestones along the way can boost your morale and reinforce your commitment to your side hustle goals.

Success is not a static destination; it's a dynamic and evolving process. Your definition of success and the metrics you use to measure it may change as your side hustle grows and evolves. Embracing flexibility and adaptability in your approach to success measurement is essential for long-term satisfaction and fulfillment.

Join us on a journey of exploration and self-discovery as we dive into the various facets of measuring success in your side hustle. Whether you aim to achieve financial independence, make a positive impact on your community, or strike a balance between work and personal life, this chapter will provide valuable insights and strategies to help you define, track, and celebrate your unique path to success.

Tracking Your Progress

In the pursuit of scaling your side hustle and achieving your aspirations, tracking your progress is a fundamental practice. It not only helps you stay motivated but also allows you to make data-driven decisions and measure your success against your goals. Effective progress tracking serves as your compass on the path to Side Hustle Millionaire status. Here's a comprehensive guide to help you understand the importance of tracking your progress and how to do it effectively:

Why Tracking Progress Matters

Clarity and Focus: Progress tracking provides clarity on where you stand in relation to your goals. It helps you stay focused on what truly matters, avoiding distractions and wasted efforts.

Motivation: Celebrating milestones and achievements along the way boosts your motivation. Tracking progress allows you to see how far you've come and reminds you of your capabilities.

Identifying Trends: It enables you to identify trends and patterns in your side hustle's performance. You can recognize what strategies work best and where adjustments are needed.

Data-Driven Decisions: Having data at your fingertips empowers you to make informed decisions. Whether it's about marketing, product development, or resource allocation, tracking progress provides valuable insights.

What to Track

- Financial Metrics: This includes revenue, profit margins, expenses, and cash flow. Financial metrics are critical indicators of your side hustle's health and growth potential.

- Customer Acquisition and Retention: Monitor the number of new customers gained and the rate at which you retain existing customers. Customer feedback and satisfaction metrics are also valuable.

- Operational Efficiency: Keep an eye on operational metrics such as production efficiency, inventory turnover, and order fulfillment time. Efficiency improvements can lead to cost savings and improved customer experience.

- Marketing Performance: Track key marketing metrics, including conversion rates, website traffic, social media engagement, and the return on investment (ROI) of your marketing campaigns.

- Product or Service Metrics: For product-based side hustles, monitor product performance, sales, and customer feedback. For service-based side hustles, track service quality, client satisfaction, and repeat business.

- Work-Life Balance: Don't forget to measure your work-life balance and well-being. High levels of stress or burnout can negatively impact your side hustle's sustainability.

How to Track Progress

- Set Specific Goals: Define clear, specific, and measurable goals. Ensure your objectives are realistic and aligned with your long-term vision.

- Use Key Performance Indicators (KPIs): Identify KPIs relevant to your side hustle's goals. KPIs are the specific metrics that matter most for measuring progress.

- Regularly Update Records: Maintain accurate records of all relevant data. Whether it's financial transactions, customer data, or marketing analytics, organized records are essential.

- Implement Tools and Software: Utilize tracking tools and software to streamline data collection and analysis. There are numerous apps and platforms available for different aspects of progress tracking.

- Create Dashboards: Consider building customized dashboards to visualize your key metrics. Dashboards provide a snapshot view of your side hustle's performance.

- Set Review Periods: Establish regular intervals for reviewing progress. Weekly, monthly, and quarterly reviews allow you to spot trends and make timely adjustments.

- Analyze and Interpret Data: Don't just collect data; analyze and interpret it. Look for patterns, anomalies, and areas where improvement is needed.

- Adjust Strategies: Based on your analysis, be prepared to adjust your strategies and tactics. Scaling often requires tweaking and refining your approaches.

Celebrate Milestones

As you track your progress, don't forget to celebrate your achievements and milestones along the way. Recognizing your successes, no matter how small, is essential for maintaining motivation and enthusiasm.

In conclusion, tracking your progress is a vital aspect of your journey to Side Hustle Millionaire status. It provides you with the insights and data needed to make informed decisions, adapt to changing circumstances, and ultimately achieve your goals. By setting clear objectives, monitoring key metrics, and regularly reviewing your progress, you'll be well-equipped to navigate the challenges and opportunities that come with scaling your side hustle.

Adjusting Your Strategy

In the dynamic world of entrepreneurship, the ability to adjust your strategy is a valuable skill on your journey to Side Hustle Millionaire status. As you scale your side hustle and face evolving challenges and opportunities, the need for flexibility and adaptability becomes increasingly apparent. Here's a comprehensive guide on why and how to adjust your strategy effectively:

The Importance of Strategy Adjustment

- Market Changes: Markets are constantly evolving, influenced by economic shifts, consumer behavior, and technological advancements. To stay relevant and competitive, your strategy must adapt to these changes.

- Competitive Landscape: New competitors may emerge, and existing ones can change their tactics. Adapting your strategy helps you maintain your position or seize opportunities in a shifting competitive landscape.

- Customer Preferences: Customer preferences and needs can evolve over time. Adjusting your strategy to align with these changes ensures that your products or services remain appealing and valuable to your target audience.
- Feedback and Data: Collecting feedback from customers and analyzing data can reveal areas where your strategy can be improved. Listening to your audience is a key driver of strategic adjustments.
- Internal Challenges: Challenges within your organization, such as resource constraints, changes in team dynamics, or operational inefficiencies, may necessitate strategy adjustments to overcome obstacles.

When to Adjust Your Strategy

- Performance Misalignment: If your side hustle is consistently falling short of its goals and key performance indicators (KPIs), it's a clear sign that your strategy may need revision.

- Market Research Insights: When market research uncovers shifts in customer behavior, emerging trends, or new opportunities, it's time to reevaluate your strategy.

- Competitive Threats: The emergence of new competitors or disruptive changes in the competitive landscape should trigger a strategic review.

- Customer Feedback: If customers provide consistent feedback about dissatisfaction with your offerings or services, consider making adjustments to address their concerns.

- Resource Reallocation: When resource allocation becomes a challenge due to financial constraints or limitations in talent, it may be necessary to realign your strategy accordingly.

How to Adjust Your Strategy

- Review Your Goals: Start by revisiting your long-term and short-term goals. Ensure they align with your current circumstances and market dynamics.

- Analyze Data: Examine data and metrics related to your side hustle's performance. Identify areas where you're falling short or excelling and use this information to inform your adjustments.

- Market Research: Stay informed about market trends, customer behavior, and industry developments. Market research can provide valuable insights for refining your strategy.

- Competitor Analysis: Evaluate the strategies of your competitors and identify gaps or opportunities that you can leverage or address in your own approach.

- Customer Feedback: Act on feedback from your customers. Address pain points and enhance aspects of your products, services, or customer experience that need improvement.

- Resource Allocation: Assess your available resources, including budget, time, and talent. Make sure your strategy aligns with your resource constraints and opportunities.

- Consult with Experts: Seek guidance from mentors, advisors, or industry experts. They can provide valuable perspectives and recommendations for adjusting your strategy.

- Scenario Planning: Consider various scenarios and their potential impacts on your side hustle. Develop contingency plans to address potential challenges and opportunities.

- Pilot and Test: Before fully implementing major strategy changes, consider piloting or testing them on a smaller scale to assess their effectiveness and gather feedback.

- Communicate Changes: If your strategy adjustments will impact customers, team members, or stakeholders, communicate the changes clearly and transparently to manage expectations.

Monitoring and Iteration

After making adjustments to your strategy, the process doesn't end there. It's essential to continuously monitor the outcomes of your changes and iterate as needed. Regularly revisit your strategy to ensure it remains aligned with your goals and the evolving business landscape.

In conclusion, adjusting your strategy is a dynamic and ongoing process essential for the growth and success of your side hustle. Embrace change as an opportunity for improvement and innovation. By staying attuned to market shifts, listening to your customers, and being flexible in your approach, you'll be well-equipped to navigate the challenges and seize the opportunities that come your way on your journey to Side Hustle Millionaire status.

Chapter 10: Case Studies

In the world of entrepreneurship and side hustles, there is no one-size-fits-all formula for success. Every journey is unique, and each side hustler faces a distinct set of challenges and opportunities. Case studies offer a valuable lens through which we can explore real-life stories of individuals who have embarked on their path to Side Hustle Millionaire status. These stories provide insights, inspiration, and practical lessons that can inform and guide your own entrepreneurial endeavors.

In this section, we will delve into a series of compelling case studies that highlight the diverse experiences and strategies of successful side hustlers. These case studies showcase individuals who have turned their passions, skills, and innovative ideas into thriving businesses. Whether they started from scratch or leveraged their existing careers, these entrepreneurs have one thing in common: they made strategic choices, adapted to changing circumstances, and navigated obstacles to reach impressive levels of success.

Through these case studies, we will uncover the pivotal decisions, creative problem-solving, and relentless determination that propelled these side hustlers toward their goals. From solo entrepreneurs to small teams, from e-commerce wizards to service providers, these stories demonstrate that there are numerous paths to success in the world of side hustles.

As you explore these case studies, consider how their experiences and lessons learned can be applied to your own journey. Whether you're in the early stages of your side hustle or looking to scale up an existing venture, these real-world examples offer valuable insights and inspiration to help you overcome challenges, seize opportunities, and ultimately achieve your aspirations of Side Hustle Millionaire status.

Success Stories of Side Hustle Millionaires

In the world of side hustles, there are extraordinary individuals who have not only balanced their full-time jobs with entrepreneurial pursuits but have also achieved remarkable success, often reaching the coveted status of Side Hustle Millionaire. These success stories serve as inspiring examples of what can be achieved through dedication, innovation, and a relentless pursuit of one's goals. In this exploration of three such stories, we'll delve into the unique journeys of individuals who transformed their side hustles into thriving businesses.

Success Story 1: Julie's Jewelry Empire

The Beginning

Julie Turner, a high school teacher with a passion for crafting jewelry, started her side hustle as a creative outlet. She designed and handcrafted unique jewelry pieces in her spare time, initially selling them at local craft fairs and through an Etsy shop. Her jewelry received positive feedback for its quality and artistic flair, laying the foundation for what would become a remarkable success story.

The Turning Point

Julie's big break came when a local boutique discovered her jewelry and approached her about consigning her pieces. This partnership not only increased her exposure but also boosted her confidence. Julie decided to take her side hustle to the next level by launching her own e-commerce store and investing in online marketing.

Scaling Up

As demand for her jewelry grew, Julie faced the challenge of maintaining quality while meeting the increasing number of orders. She hired a small team of skilled artisans to assist with production. Julie's meticulous attention to detail ensured that her handcrafted pieces maintained their unique charm.

Achieving Side Hustle Millionaire Status

Julie's e-commerce store, along with a strong social media presence, attracted a loyal customer base. Her side hustle transformed into a full-fledged jewelry empire. In five years, she achieved Side Hustle Millionaire status, with her business generating seven figures in annual revenue. Julie's story highlights the potential of turning a passion into a profitable enterprise with the right strategy, dedication, and commitment to quality.

Success Story 2: Mark's Tech Innovation

The Start

Mark Anderson, a software engineer at a tech company, always had a knack for coding and developing software solutions. His side hustle began as a hobby project – creating mobile apps in his free time. One of his apps, a unique productivity tool, gained attention for its innovative approach to task management.

The Breakthrough

Mark decided to offer his app on app stores for a nominal fee, and its popularity began to soar. Positive user reviews and word-of-mouth recommendations helped him gain traction. Mark recognized the app's potential and made the bold decision to leave his full-time job to focus on his side hustle.

Expansion and Innovation

With newfound time and dedication, Mark continued to refine his app and develop new features. He also expanded his portfolio of apps, targeting various niches. His dedication to user experience and continuous improvement resulted in a growing user base and a strong brand reputation.

Reaching Side Hustle Millionaire Status

Mark's apps became a global success, generating substantial revenue through app sales and in-app purchases. Within seven years, he reached Side Hustle Millionaire status, showcasing the transformative power of innovative tech solutions and the courage to pursue one's passion.

Success Story 3: Lisa's Online Learning Empire

The Beginning

Lisa Martinez, a college professor, possessed a deep love for teaching and a desire to share knowledge beyond the classroom. She began creating online courses related to her field of expertise, initially as a way to supplement her income. Her courses covered a wide range of topics, from academic subjects to personal development.

Recognition and Growth

Lisa's engaging teaching style and the quality of her content led to rave reviews and high enrollments in her online courses. Recognizing the potential of online education, she devoted more time to her side hustle, creating a comprehensive library of courses.

The Pivot

As the demand for online learning surged, Lisa decided to pivot her side hustle into a full-time business. She invested in professional video production, enhanced her course offerings, and created a subscription-based model that provided access to her entire course catalog.

Side Hustle Millionaire in Education

Lisa's online learning empire expanded rapidly. Her commitment to delivering high-quality education attracted students from around the world. Within a decade, Lisa achieved Side Hustle Millionaire status, not only transforming her life but also impacting the lives of countless learners worldwide. Her story underscores the potential of online education and the ability to monetize expertise in a digital age.

Key Takeaways

These three success stories of Side Hustle Millionaires highlight several common themes:

- Passion and Expertise: Each entrepreneur leveraged their passion and expertise to create unique products or services.
- Adaptability: They were open to adapting their strategies, whether through partnerships, expanding their offerings, or embracing digital platforms.
- Quality and Innovation: Maintaining a commitment to quality and constantly innovating played a pivotal role in their success.

- Courage and Dedication: All three individuals displayed the courage to take risks, make bold decisions, and dedicate substantial time and effort to their side hustles.
- Impact: Their success stories are not just about financial gains but also the positive impact they had on their customers, clients, or learners.

Aspiring entrepreneurs can draw inspiration and lessons from these stories, understanding that Side Hustle Millionaire status is attainable through passion, innovation, and unwavering dedication to one's vision. Each journey is unique, but the principles of entrepreneurship and the potential for success remain constant.

Chapter 11: Planning for the Future

In the world of side hustles and entrepreneurial pursuits, the present is a canvas upon which we paint our ambitions, but the future is the frame that gives our efforts purpose and direction. Planning for the future is an essential practice for individuals striving to reach Side Hustle Millionaire status. It involves setting clear goals, making strategic decisions, and developing a roadmap that guides your entrepreneurial journey toward long-term success.

In this section, we will explore the importance of planning for the future in the context of your side hustle. We'll delve into the following key aspects:

- Goal Setting: Defining your aspirations and objectives is the foundational step in planning for the future. Your goals serve as the compass that points you in the right direction, motivating you to push boundaries and overcome challenges.

- Strategic Decision-Making: Strategic decisions are the building blocks of your side hustle's growth. They encompass choices related to product development, marketing strategies, resource allocation, and scalability.

- Risk Management: Entrepreneurship inherently involves risk. Planning for the future includes identifying potential risks and developing mitigation strategies to safeguard your side hustle's sustainability.

- Financial Planning: Sound financial planning is critical for achieving long-term success. This involves budgeting, saving, and making informed financial decisions to support your side hustle's growth.

- Market Analysis: Understanding market trends, customer behavior, and industry dynamics is essential for making informed decisions and staying ahead of the competition.

- Scaling Strategies: If your goal is to scale your side hustle, you'll need a clear plan for expansion. This includes considerations for hiring, infrastructure, and operational efficiency.

- Adaptability: The ability to adapt to changing circumstances and pivot when necessary is a hallmark of successful entrepreneurs. Planning for the future should also include contingencies for unforeseen challenges or opportunities.

- Long-Term Vision: Beyond short-term objectives, planning for the future entails crafting a long-term vision for your side hustle. This vision provides a sense of purpose and guides your strategic efforts over the years.

Your side hustle is not merely a means to supplement your income; it's an avenue for realizing your dreams and aspirations. Effective planning for the future ensures that your side hustle remains aligned with your goals and continues to evolve as you progress on your entrepreneurial journey.

Join us as we explore the strategies, tools, and insights necessary for planning for the future of your side hustle. Whether your ambition is to generate significant income, make a positive impact, or achieve a fulfilling work-life balance, this section will provide valuable guidance to help you chart a course toward a successful and sustainable future.

Investing Your Profits

One of the key objectives in your journey toward Side Hustle Millionaire status is not just earning money but making that money work for you. Investing your profits strategically is a critical step in building long-term wealth and financial security. In this chapter, we will explore the importance of investing your side hustle earnings and offer insights into how to do it effectively.

The Power of Investing

Investing is a means of allocating your capital to assets or ventures with the expectation of generating returns or increasing value over time. It's a financial strategy that extends the potential of your earnings far beyond what you can achieve through savings alone. Here's why investing your profits is crucial:

- Wealth Accumulation: Investing allows you to grow your wealth over time by generating passive income, capital appreciation, or both.

- Beat Inflation: Inflation erodes the purchasing power of your money over time. Investments have the potential to outpace inflation, preserving and even increasing your real wealth.

- Financial Freedom: Successful investments can provide financial stability, allowing you to achieve financial milestones, such as retirement or funding major life goals.

- Diversification: Investing allows you to spread your risk across different asset classes, reducing the impact of poor performance in any one area.

Where to Invest Your Profits

The investment landscape offers various opportunities to grow your money. Here are some common investment options to consider:

- Stock Market: Investing in individual stocks or exchange-traded funds (ETFs) provides ownership in companies and the potential for capital appreciation and dividends.
- Real Estate: Real estate can be an attractive investment, offering rental income and property value appreciation over time.
- Bonds: Bonds are fixed-income securities that provide regular interest payments and return the principal amount at maturity.
- Mutual Funds: These investment vehicles pool money from multiple investors to invest in a diversified portfolio of stocks, bonds, or other assets.

- Startups and Ventures: If you have industry expertise, consider investing in startups or entrepreneurial ventures where your knowledge can provide an edge.

- Retirement Accounts: Contribute to tax-advantaged retirement accounts such as 401(k)s or IRAs to benefit from tax-deferred or tax-free growth.

- Peer-to-Peer Lending: Platforms allow you to lend money to individuals or small businesses in exchange for interest payments.

- Cryptocurrencies: Cryptocurrencies like Bitcoin and Ethereum have gained popularity as speculative investments with potential for high returns.

Strategies for Effective Investing

Investing can be both rewarding and challenging. Here are strategies to help you make the most of your side hustle profits:

- Diversify: Spread your investments across different asset classes to reduce risk. A diversified portfolio can help weather market volatility.
- Invest for the Long Term: Consider a long-term perspective when investing. Compound interest and long-term growth potential can significantly boost your wealth.
- Set Clear Goals: Define your investment goals, whether it's retirement, a major purchase, or passive income. Your goals will shape your investment strategy.
- Stay Informed: Keep abreast of market trends and stay informed about your investments. Knowledge is a valuable asset in the investment world.
- Seek Professional Advice: If you're unsure about investment decisions, consult a financial advisor who can provide personalized guidance.

- Automate Investments: Set up automated contributions to your investment accounts to ensure consistent savings and investment.
- Monitor and Adjust: Regularly review your investments and make adjustments as needed. A well-maintained portfolio aligns with your goals and risk tolerance.

Risk and Reward

It's important to acknowledge that all investments carry some level of risk. The potential for higher returns often comes with higher risk. When investing your side hustle profits, assess your risk tolerance and consider a diversified approach to manage risk effectively.

In conclusion, investing your side hustle profits is a powerful strategy for achieving your financial goals and building long-term wealth. It's not just about earning money; it's about making your money work for you. By understanding your investment options, setting clear goals, and employing sound investment strategies, you can harness the potential of your side hustle earnings to secure a brighter financial future.

Preparing for Financial Independence

Financial independence is a goal that many aspire to achieve, and your side hustle can be a powerful tool to help you reach that milestone. It's not just about having enough money to cover your expenses; it's about having the freedom to make choices without being constrained by financial concerns. In this chapter, we will explore the concept of financial independence, why it matters, and how you can prepare for it through your side hustle.

What is Financial Independence?

Financial independence, often referred to as FI, is a state where your financial resources are sufficient to support your desired lifestyle without relying on traditional employment or a regular paycheck. It means having the freedom to make choices based on your preferences and values, rather than financial necessity. Achieving financial independence provides peace of mind and opens up opportunities for personal fulfillment.

Why Financial Independence Matters

- Freedom: Financial independence gives you the freedom to pursue your passions, travel, or take on new challenges without worrying about money.

- Reduced Stress: It reduces financial stress and anxiety, allowing you to focus on what truly matters to you.

- Early Retirement: FI can enable early retirement, giving you more time to enjoy life and pursue activities you're passionate about.

- Generational Impact: Achieving financial independence can positively impact your family and future generations by providing financial security and opportunities.

- How Your Side Hustle Can Prepare You for FI
- Your side hustle can be a powerful catalyst for achieving financial independence. Here's how it can contribute to your journey:
- Income Generation: Your side hustle generates additional income streams, which can accelerate your progress toward FI.
- Savings and Investments: The profits from your side hustle can be channeled into savings and investments, helping you build a financial cushion.
- Debt Reduction: Extra income can be used to pay down debts, reducing financial burdens and freeing up more of your resources.
- Skill Development: Your side hustle may involve acquiring valuable skills that can lead to higher-paying opportunities or entrepreneurial ventures.
- Steps to Prepare for Financial Independence

- Set Clear Financial Goals: Define your financial independence goals, including how much you need to achieve them and your desired timeline.

- Create a Budget: Develop a comprehensive budget that tracks your income, expenses, and savings. Identify areas where you can cut costs and increase savings.

- Maximize Side Hustle Income: Continuously work on growing your side hustle income through strategic planning, marketing efforts, and expansion.

- Build an Emergency Fund: Establish an emergency fund to cover unexpected expenses and prevent setbacks on your FI journey.

- Invest Wisely: Invest your savings wisely to generate passive income. Consider a diversified portfolio of investments, including stocks, bonds, and real estate.

- Reduce Debt: Prioritize paying off high-interest debts, such as credit card balances or personal loans, to free up more of your income for savings and investments.

- Monitor Your Progress: Regularly review your financial situation and adjust your strategies as needed. Celebrate milestones along the way.
- Plan for Healthcare and Insurance: Ensure you have adequate healthcare coverage and insurance plans in place to protect your financial stability in case of unexpected medical expenses or emergencies.

The Road to Financial Independence

Financial independence is a journey, not a destination. It requires discipline, planning, and determination. Your side hustle is a valuable asset on this journey, providing you with the means to accelerate your progress and achieve greater financial security.

As you prepare for financial independence through your side hustle, remember that the path may have its ups and downs, but the ultimate reward is the freedom to live life on your own terms. Stay committed to your goals, stay informed about personal finance, and seek advice from financial professionals when necessary. Financial independence is within reach, and your side hustle can be the vehicle that gets you there.

Conclusion

Congratulations on embarking on a journey toward achieving a 10x income goal through your side hustle! This ambitious pursuit of financial growth and entrepreneurial success reflects your determination and vision for a brighter future. As we wrap up this chapter, let's recap some essential takeaways and parting insights to guide you on your path to Side Hustle Millionaire status.

Your vision for financial success and independence is the driving force behind your side hustle journey. Embrace this vision and keep it at the forefront of your efforts. Visualize the life you aspire to lead, the impact you want to make, and the freedom you seek. Your vision will serve as a constant source of motivation, pushing you forward during challenges and setbacks.

A 10x income goal is ambitious, but it's within reach with the right strategies and dedication. Break this lofty goal into smaller, actionable milestones. These smaller goals serve as stepping stones, allowing you to track your progress and celebrate your achievements along the way. Regularly review and adjust your goals as your side hustle evolves.

Your side hustle is more than just a means of generating extra income. It's a platform for personal and financial growth, a canvas for your creativity, and a vehicle for turning your passions into profit. Approach your side hustle with dedication and a commitment to excellence. Continuously seek ways to improve and innovate in your niche.

Entrepreneurship is a dynamic journey filled with uncertainties. Be prepared to adapt to changing circumstances, whether they come in the form of market shifts, competition, or personal challenges. Flexibility and resilience are essential traits that will help you navigate the ever-evolving entrepreneurial landscape.

In the pursuit of your 10x income goal, never stop learning. Stay curious, seek knowledge, and invest in your personal and professional development. The skills you acquire along the way can be invaluable assets in your side hustle journey.

Financial discipline and prudent management of your earnings are vital. Create a budget, build an emergency fund, and reduce high-interest debts to secure your financial stability. Invest your profits wisely to generate passive income streams that can support your long-term goals, including financial independence.

Don't underestimate the power of community and support networks. Surround yourself with like-minded individuals, mentors, and advisors who can provide guidance, inspiration, and valuable insights. The entrepreneurial journey can be solitary at times, but you're not alone in your pursuit of success.

Amid the hustle and hard work, remember to celebrate your achievements, no matter how small they may seem. Recognizing your progress and milestones is essential for maintaining motivation and sustaining your commitment to your 10x income goal.

Persistence is the key to overcoming challenges and setbacks. Expect hurdles along the way, but view them as opportunities to learn and grow. Your ability to persevere in the face of adversity will ultimately determine your success.

Lastly, cultivate a Side Hustle Millionaire mindset. This mindset combines ambition, discipline, creativity, and a willingness to take calculated risks. It's about seeing your side hustle not as a mere hobby but as a vehicle for achieving significant financial and personal growth.

In closing, your pursuit of a 10x income goal through your side hustle is an inspiring journey of self-discovery, ambition, and resilience. It's a path that promises not only financial rewards but also personal fulfillment and freedom. Remember that success is not measured solely by the destination but by the progress you make and the positive impact you create along the way.

Continue to dream big, set bold goals, and work tirelessly toward your vision of financial independence. Your side hustle has the potential to transform your life and open doors to a world of opportunities. Embrace the challenges, relish the successes, and always believe in your ability to achieve greatness.

As you move forward, know that your dedication and determination will propel you closer to your 10x income goal, and perhaps even beyond it. The path to Side Hustle Millionaire status is challenging, but it's also incredibly rewarding. Your journey has just begun, and the future holds endless possibilities. So, step confidently into that future, and let your side hustle be the vehicle that takes you there.

Your Path to Side Hustle Millionaire Status

Becoming a Side Hustle Millionaire is a journey that requires determination, strategy, and a mindset geared towards success. It's not just about earning extra income; it's about creating a sustainable and lucrative source of wealth that can transform your financial future. As we explore the path to Side Hustle Millionaire status, let's delve into the essential steps and key principles that will guide you on this extraordinary journey.

1. Define Your Vision

Every successful journey begins with a clear vision of your destination. Define what "millionaire status" means to you. Is it financial freedom, early retirement, or the ability to pursue your passions without financial constraints? Your vision will serve as your guiding star, motivating you to push forward, even when faced with challenges.

2. Set Ambitious Goals

With your vision in mind, set ambitious yet achievable goals. Break down your journey into smaller, actionable steps and milestones. These goals will provide you with a roadmap to follow and allow you to track your progress along the way. Remember, your 10x income goal is the overarching target, but the journey comprises numerous smaller victories.

3. Choose the Right Side Hustle

Selecting the right side hustle is crucial. It should align with your skills, interests, and market demand. Whether it's e-commerce, freelancing, consulting, or a creative endeavor, your side hustle should be a platform for turning your talents into profit. Continuously assess and refine your side hustle to maximize its income potential.

4. Invest in Skill Development

Success in the side hustle world often depends on your skills and knowledge. Invest time and effort in developing the necessary skills, whether it's digital marketing, coding, sales, or any other expertise relevant to your venture. Lifelong learning is a cornerstone of entrepreneurial success.

5. Build a Strong Brand

Your brand is your identity in the market. Invest in building a strong and memorable brand for your side hustle. This includes creating a professional online presence, crafting a unique value proposition, and delivering exceptional quality in your products or services. A strong brand attracts loyal customers and sets you apart from the competition.

6. Market and Promote Effectively

Marketing is the engine that drives your side hustle's growth. Develop a comprehensive marketing strategy that leverages various channels, from social media and content marketing to paid advertising and email campaigns. Understand your target audience and tailor your messaging to their needs and preferences.

7. Manage Finances Wisely

Financial management is the backbone of your journey to Side Hustle Millionaire status. Create a budget, monitor your income and expenses, and make informed financial decisions. Allocate a portion of your earnings to savings and investments to ensure long-term financial security and growth.

8. Scale Thoughtfully

Scaling your side hustle requires strategic planning. Consider factors such as hiring additional help, expanding product lines, or entering new markets. Scaling should align with your goals and your capacity to maintain quality and customer satisfaction.

9. Stay Adaptable

The entrepreneurial journey is dynamic and unpredictable. Be prepared to adapt to changing circumstances, seize opportunities, and pivot when necessary. Adaptability is a trait shared by many successful side hustlers.

10. Seek Mentorship and Support

Don't hesitate to seek guidance from mentors, industry experts, or entrepreneurial communities. Learning from others' experiences and insights can provide valuable shortcuts to success and help you avoid common pitfalls.

11. Celebrate Milestones

As you progress on your journey, celebrate your achievements, no matter how small they may seem. Recognizing your progress boosts motivation and reinforces your commitment to your goals.

12. Maintain a Positive Mindset

Your mindset is a powerful tool in achieving Side Hustle Millionaire status. Cultivate a positive and resilient mindset that allows you to overcome setbacks and stay focused on your vision.

13. Never Stop Learning

Finally, embrace the philosophy of lifelong learning. Stay curious, stay informed, and stay open to new opportunities. The world of side hustles and entrepreneurship is constantly evolving, and your ability to adapt and grow will be your greatest asset.

Your path to Side Hustle Millionaire status is an extraordinary journey filled with challenges, triumphs, and personal growth. Embrace it with enthusiasm, commitment, and unwavering belief in your potential. Remember, the road may be long, but the destination is worth every step. Your journey has already begun, and the future holds limitless possibilities. So, take that first step with confidence, and let your side hustle be the catalyst that propels you to Side Hustle Millionaire status.